Tia Talks

Tia Talks

My Life in a Multi-breed Family

Lesley Osborn

LCC nPrint

LCC nPrint
Publication Service of Lanham Creative Content
Fort Mill, South Carolina

ISBN 979-8-9874807-0-0 (pbk.)
ISBN 979-8-9874807-1-7 (ebook)

Cover design by Gary J. Lanham
Lanham Creative Content, LLC

Contents

DEDICATION

Tia Talks – My Life in a Multi-breed Family is dedicated to my mother and father.

To my mom, who, for fifty years, bred and exhibited English Setters under the kennel name of Canberra.

And to my father, who, first and foremost, instilled in me the talent and love for writing. He often told his colleagues that putting up with all the many "Tia's" in the household was cheaper than a psychiatrist for Grandma.

Credit also goes to the various members of the GREYSETT household and its changing complexion over the years. These characters have inspired this book.

Thanks for making this house a happy home.

PREFACE

Tia Talks began as a monthly column I wrote for the national newsletter of the English Setter Association of America.

Those were the days when many writers still used typewriters. Remember those? I was cutting edge and used a computer. A big one. And back then, everything relied on snail mail. So, I wrote my column and sent it on its way with the postman.

When I wrote *Tia Talks,* the newsletter was a paper version mailed to the membership. As many things change over time, so did that newsletter. Today it is digital.

As Tia aged, she had less interaction with the other canine members of our family. Her monthly column aged along with her until I decided to bring it to a close. Tia remained with us for a while longer until she peacefully crossed The Bridge.

As I wrote the column, I kept every printed page safe in a binder. I still have them. I never imagined that after all these years her column would become a book. *Her* book.

The stories Tia shared in her column are those you are reading today.

Tia was certainly a character back then, and she remains a well-loved memory in the hearts of GREYSETT.

I am immensely gratified to share her life and stories with you.

Lesley Osborn
Ocala, Florida
December 2022

Author's Introduction

Before you start reading

You can watch Lesley talk about the origin of GREYSETT, *Tia Talks*, and her series, ***My Dogs Talk***.

Just scan the QR code below.

PROLOGUE

"Who ate the dining room table?" bellowed Grandma. "Well, it certainly wasn't me! I'm lucky that I have any teeth left in my mouth at my age!"

Tia Talks is the story of a thirteen-year-old English Setter who lives in a household with multiple other canines and four birds. Oh yes, let's not forget Aunt Lesley's thoroughbred, Calli. Thank God she lives on a farm in another county.

Grandma brought Tia to South Florida from Canada when she was just a pup and lovingly raised her. Grandma and Aunt Lesley lived together, sharing all the responsibilities of running the household. Aunt Lesley loved Tia; however, they had a rather adversarial relationship at times.

This relationship is evidenced throughout the book.

Tia has seen the household change in many ways over the years, and somehow, she keeps on ticking. The faces keep changing, and Tia rolls with the punches. At least, she gives it her best effort. Grandma decided to retire. Where did she drag everyone to? Ocala, Florida.

When Tia arrived, she quickly learned that she now lived in THE HORSE CAPITAL OF THE WORLD. Nothing surprises her anymore. Just when she thought that she'd seen it all, Aunt Lesley went out and rescued a horse!

When Tia moved to Ocala, she assumed that she would be retiring right along with Grandma. Much to her dismay, Sophie showed up. When Sophie took a fancy to Milo, Thunder, and Chloe, life in the GREYSETT household would never be the same. Any plans for quiet, peaceful days for Tia flew right out the window the day that crossbreed puppy arrived!

It's like Tia's said all along: "I just can't win!"

• 1 •

Bonjour

Bonjour and welcome.

My name is Tia, and I am the newest member of the GREYSETT household.

I hail from somewhere up in Canada. I guess that makes me French. A French English Setter–now that's class!

This book is by me, about me, and for me.

It was a major move to relocate myself to South Florida, especially for someone as sweet and innocent as "MOI!!" The problem is, out of everyone in the house, the only one who ever seems to be in trouble is me. I can't help it if I have an agenda and the others don't.

Let me tell you about my roommates.

First is Alex, the queen mother English Setter, and her daughter, Kate, who defers to everyone. Then there's Willow, the queen mother Whippet, and her sister, Ruby, who also defers to everyone.

Finally, and down on the size chart is Bridget, the queen mother Doxie, and her three Doxie brothers: Bandit, Beau, and Casey. They're all chickens also. Get the picture? Three queens, three sizes, one household—I don't stand a chance!!

As the newest family member, I get blamed for everything that happens around here. Take, for example, the thirty-year-old coffee table. It was already distressed. I didn't think they'd notice. Guess again. Grandma gave me a timeout session in my crate. She left me there well over the therapeutic limit of ten minutes.

Besides, she keeps waving this thing around called a plane ticket.

Destination?

Anywhere!

• 2 •

I Dare You!

Well, I'm still here, but Grandma changed my name to Tia Knock It Off.

I wonder why.

Oh, alright, I'll tell you why. I'm yelled at all day long. Everyone in the neighborhood knows my name. Listen, I live in the heart of squirrel country.

They hang by their tails, do tricks, and call my name. It's unnatural not to bark at squirrels. Grandma thinks I don't hear her on the phone telling all of you that I'm a hysterical barker, that she hasn't had one like me in thirty years. She did some research on these things called bark collars.

She polled the entire national English Setter community. All of you said, "Yes, yes, get it."

She got it!

At first, she wanted to buy a citronella collar, which sounded pretty good to me. Well, until Aunt Lesley thought of filling it with nitrous oxide.

Grandma ended up ordering the kind that delivers a shock big enough to cause a power surge in the house. I must give credit where credit is due. It did take her several days to show me that thing.

"Come near me with that," I said, "and I promise, I'll never show again."

By the way, did I forget to mention that Grandma purchased me with her high hopes for me growing up to become a beautiful show dog? Okay, so I haven't been in the ring yet, but just wait until The Specialty. She'll be sorry.

After several days of deliberation, she finally got up the nerve to try it on me, without the shock turned on. She says she's waiting until I'm out of control. She's more scared than I am.

So, the day finally arrives. She puts the collar on me. I'm out of control, and she turns on that shocker thing.

Hey! It's too big–it slides off my neck.

It's useless.

IT DOESN'T WORK!!

I've been granted a pardon.

AT LEAST FOR A WHILE.

• 3 •

Thanksgiving Vacation

Aunt Lesley and Grandma have a steadfast rule: they never go on vacation at the same time and leave us home alone. Because that would mean that we would have to be boarded in a strange facility.

Heaven forbid we should get a break from the mundane life we lead and venture out into the world for a change.

What would be so terrible?

Casey might lose a few pounds?

Thanksgiving was upon us, and Aunt Lesley's brother invited her and Grandma for a visit to Kansas (finally). After much deliberation—and a new will and testament drawn up that made provisions for all of us—we were all going on holiday to camp.

Or so we thought.

Departure day arrived, and we all piled into the van with eager anticipation of our new adventure. The van pulled into the boarding kennel, and we all disembarked. We registered at the front desk, got our room assignments, and proceeded to check out the accommodations.

Everything had seemed okay until Casey, the fat Doxie, asked, "Where's my bed?"

"What do you mean, that mat on the floor? I only sleep on four-hundred-thread-count sheets. Pink ones."

"Sheets? What are sheets?" I asked.

“Well, they’re these crisp, clean, pink things with gingham checks, and they go on the bed. We all sleep under them at night.”

“Bed?” I asked again. “I don’t understand.”

“When Grandma says, ‘Okay, we’re going out for errands, let’s go to bed,’ all of us big guys run into the kennel and our crates with our mats.”

“Aren’t those beds?” I asked Casey.

“Well, maybe for you guys, but when Aunt Lesley calls us to bed at night, didn’t you ever wonder where we four little Doxies go?”

Over the gate and down the hall,
  first door on the right.
That is where you’ll find us all,
  four tucked in for the night.

"Hey, Aunt Lesley, it's me. Tia. Tia in the kennel. Can we talk?"

• 4 •

Beginner's Luck

Before Grandma decided she'd enter me in my first dog show, a number of things needed to be done.

I had to have a vet take a picture of me; I think they called it an X-ray.

(Wait until Aunt Lesley hears that all my parts are perfect. I'll make a show dog after all. Now she'll have to let me stay.)

I had to be trimmed in places where I didn't know I had hair. And bathed, combed, and dried until I couldn't stand up anymore.

Grandma and Aunt Lesley stuffed me with food. By stuffed, I mean just like they do to a turkey before Thanksgiving.

And then I had to go to bed early.

Now I was ready to go to my first dog show.

It was awful.

I couldn't bring my best pal, Kate, along for moral support. I had to go alone. I threw up in my crate twice, and it was only a twenty-minute drive.

Once there, Grandma handed me over to a total stranger, called a professional handler. I kept trying to remember everything she taught me.

Hold your head up.

Don't brace.

Stay stacked.

And look happy.

"Okay, I can do that," I thought.

And then someone they called "THE JUDGE" came near me.

I almost died.

But I bit the bullet, practiced my breathing, and managed to bring home a blue ribbon—first in my class of one.

I guess I'm finally a show dog.

Now, if only I could do it again tomorrow.

I did it! I won!

I won my 1st point!

Who would have thought: ME—perfect parts and a point!

"Oh, Aunt Lesley."

• 5 •

The Bold and The Beautiful

I had my first real photoshoot today. Okay, so there was no wardrobe and makeup. No lights, camera, or action. And the shoot was shot by Aunt Lesley with a Kodak in the den.

A girl can dream, can't she?

There is more action going on in our den than just picture taking.

You see, Bridget has staked out her territory in Grandma's lap.

Now, I don't mind. Really, I don't. Bridget only takes up seventeen pounds worth of lap. That leaves more than enough for me.

What irks me is that she's Aunt Lesley's Doxie, so what's she doing in Grandma's lap?

Especially at eleven o'clock at night when I need a little bonding?

Let her get in her own mother's lap!

Well, if looks could kill!!

Her eyes get black, and so help me they seem to change direction right in their sockets.

Her neck goes up like a periscope and she gets so stiff, it's as if rigor mortis has set in.

I try to be friendly, but her body language shouts words not fit to print. Frankly, I think the old girl's jealous.

The camera loves me, and she has crooked legs.

So, she sleeps on those darned sheets. So what?

Has Walt Disney offered her a contract?

I don't think so.

They haven't offered me one either, but I'll never tell.

• 6 •

DEPARTURE DAY

It was six o'clock in the morning - Departure Day for the Specialty - and Grandma's luggage was all lined up in the hall. It was great when my ride fell through, and I didn't have to go.

But then it dawned on me; we'd all be home alone with Aunt Lesley. What did she have in store for us?

Especially me—she hates me!

An icy chill ran up my spine. I overheard promises made by Aunt Lesley.

I'd be fattened up.

Kate would learn to stay out of everyone's lap.

And Alex would go through detox and be roll-free by the time Grandma got home.

I shuddered to think of what lay ahead of us. As the taxi left, we waved goodbye.

And I prayed.

On Monday, the gate that keeps us out of the rest of the house fell, and Aunt Lesley didn't know how to fix it.

"Oh boy," I thought. "Field trips through the house for a week!"

No such luck because she jammed it into place.

Tuesday was uneventful. I ate on my own, Kate stayed on the floor, and Alex didn't have any rolls, just a large box of dog biscuits.

On Wednesday, Aunt Lesley came down with the flu, and I caught a bird. As she came running outside in her robe with a beach towel, I looked up, and the bird flew away.

On Thursday, I got yelled at for growling at Beau over a bowl of roast pork lo mein.

Friday was a safe day.

On Saturday, I came nose to nose with a giant, fat, juicy toad—any dog parent's worst nightmare.

On Sunday, Beau tried to bite my face during a thunderstorm.

Grandma will be home tomorrow. Boy, will we be glad.

I gained a few ounces, Kate is still climbing into laps, and Alex is now roll-free (but heavier by three large boxes of biscuits.)

Well, two out of three aren't bad.

But, most of all, I do believe that Aunt Lesley will be glad when Grandma is home, even though she'll never admit it.

It was a big responsibility to take care of us - especially me.

Just between you and me, I'm no walk in the park...

• 7 •

A Hurricane's A Comin'

It was headed straight for us.

Aunt Lesley and Grandma sat glued to the television day and night, watching the weather reports.

Aunt Lesley began her yearly hurricane preparations. She stocks up on ravioli every year, but this storm was bigger than ravioli.

Yes, every day, for five days (sometimes twice a day as her nerves dictated), she ran to the grocery store to stock up on food and other necessities. For some reason, her purchases included some forty-eight rolls of toilet tissue—just in case. She believes in being prepared.

With each trip to the store, the shelves emptied.

First to go, of course, was the bottled water. Now, we already had forty gallons of Zephyrhills water sitting in the garage. (After all, we had to drink also.)

Since there was no water to be had, she stocked up on juice, every kind she could grab off the shelf before the next person.

Aunt Lesley even brought home a supply of Pepsi that could quench the thirst of one hundred people, which wouldn't have been so bad except that neither she nor Grandma drank Pepsi.

In desperation, she made one last trip to the store the day before the hurricane was due to strike.

She bought whatever was left:

yams (institutional size);

green beans (which she hates);

dinosaur-shaped macaroni in cans (the kind that kids eat);

large-size cans of pork and beans;

and reduced-fat peanut butter.

She also stocked up on plenty of energy foods to fight off the storm—Yodels (her favorite), Drake's cakes, cookies, and pies.

She forgot nothing.

She even brought in a supply of Pepcid and Imodium. You know, just in case.

While Aunt Lesley was buying out Publix, Grandma was buying out Pet Supermarket.

She figured two hundred pounds of dry dog food and fifty cans of Pedigree would be enough. And she placed it all in the living room, right next to those forty-eight rolls of toilet paper.

Now, the dry food, she thought, would not go to waste. After all, we ate it every night.

Then Grandma opened a bag. They changed the recipe! And we wouldn't eat it!

Their last mission was a trip to Walmart to buy a Sterno stove (to cook those yams). They got a cooler and some ice packs to store Alex's extra insulin for her diabetes.

Now finally finished, there was food and supplies stacked everywhere.

The storm grew closer.

It was time to bring in anything that wasn't nailed down. Plants, porch furniture, the birds, bicycles – you name it, and it was in the living room right next to the toilet paper and the two hundred pounds of dog food that nobody would eat. All that remained outside was the spa.

Exhausted but ready, they both sat by the TV, waiting and watching the weather channel. We were, too; however, we couldn't understand what all the fuss was about.

8 p.m.

9 p.m.

10 p.m. and the storm grew closer.

11 p.m., 12 a.m., and 1 a.m. came and went.

It was nerve-wracking, and finally, Aunt Lesley couldn't wait any longer. She had to break open the Yodels!

By 5 a.m., the storm had turned, and it completely missed us.

Relieved, yet frustrated because of all the work she'd done, Aunt Lesley immediately went on a Yodel binge.

Well, as the storm moved past us and traveled up the coast, she and Grandma began to take stock and decide just what to do with all their supplies.

The dog food could be exchanged.

And the toilet paper would, how does one delicately say, be used?

But, neither of them had a plan for those yams.

Well, one thing's for sure–they were all ready for Y2K...

• 8 •

OCALA OR BUST

Our house in south Florida sold in record time, and Aunt Lesley and Grandma had a new house waiting for us in Ocala, Florida. At last—a quiet place for me to retire.

Well, this was no easy task.

Thirty years' worth of stuff had to be sorted through and either discarded or packed. To make matters worse, a storm was brewing somewhere off the coast of Africa. The Miami Hurricane Center was watching it carefully, and so were Aunt Lesley and Grandma.

They worked day and night for weeks. "This stays, that goes" was all I heard. I'm lucky that I got fed. The closing dates on the house came and went several times causing them to lose the moving van reservations a few times.

There were other considerations also. There were nine of us. Grandma's car was going on the moving van, which left Aunt Lesley's big Toyota. That meant some of us had to be transported to Ocala by friends from the greyhound adoption kennel in their big bus. Those plans would be fine with me if I wasn't one of them! I'd better be one of those going up in that Toyota!

Four of our canine family were already boarded at the greyhound kennel getting them out from underfoot. Lucky me; I stayed home along with two neurotic Doxies (Casey and Zachary), Daniel (one of the greyhounds), and Kate (another English

Setter.) We were the five chosen to travel in the Toyota along with the four birds.

Moving day finally arrived. Naturally, it was pouring. And the movers arrived late.

The moving crew loaded their van in the rain, then departed. Finally, after checking and rechecking for anything that might have been left behind, we loaded up everything that didn't go on the moving van. Finally, Aunt Lesley, Grandma, me, the four other dogs—along with our four birds—pulled away from the house at 7 p.m. in the pouring rain.

The trip was a nightmare.

Aunt Lesley's two Doxies weren't too bad, but Daniel cried for the entire trip! He's the world's worst traveler, but he's Grandma's "heart dog," so, of course, he had to come in the car. Kate has diabetes and needs insulin every time her levels go out of whack from stress. And considering the amount of stress in that Toyota that night, she needed it several times.

Aunt Lesley had just purchased this huge Toyota 4 Runner and didn't know how to operate anything. She hadn't bothered to read the owner's manual, much to Grandma's dismay. (She reads the directions to everything.)

It was dark. And it was raining. And we were lost.

Grandma couldn't read the map in the dark. She pushed the first button she could find to turn on the inside lights. Well, the sunroof opened!

The rain came in, and the birds began to fly around their travel cages, which excited Kate and me. We are bird dogs, after all. Grandma began to search for the owner's manual. Ten minutes later, after pulling off I-95 in the dark and heavy traffic, she figured it out. The two of them weren't speaking, but we were all on our way again.

What should have been a four-hour drive took almost seven hours. We all had to make stops for "you know what" and at different times, no less. Aunt Lesley and Grandma constantly needed coffee and doughnuts to stay awake. Exhausted, we finally arrived in Ocala in the middle of the night. They opened the door to our new home, finding it filled with a sea of boxes.

The movers had arrived before us and unloaded everything. It was raining, there were no lights, and neither Aunt Lesley nor Grandma was there to supervise. All the boxes had been marked clearly, but the crew didn't seem to care. So, in it all went, just as it came off the truck. Those movers just put stuff anywhere they felt like it.

Aunt Lesley and Grandma found a few lamps and plugged them in. Next, they fed us. And after that, they put us out to exercise. (Thank goodness Grandma already had the fencing installed). Then, at last, we all went to bed.

We were up at dawn. And things looked even worse than the night before.

Zachary (who can barely walk as it is) kept getting lost behind all the boxes. The house was huge, and the layout was different than our old house. So, we all kept getting lost. What did Grandma care about? That we all learned where the back door was, which led out to the fenced property!

Two days later, the other dogs arrived. Our family was again complete. And Aunt Lesley and Grandma wallowed in self-pity for a few days before getting to work on those boxes.

Two years later, all are finally unpacked, no thanks to Aunt Lesley. Grandma did most of it herself. She claims that Aunt Lesley slept through the whole thing!

• 9 •

DINNER FOR EIGHT

When the clock strikes 6 p.m., two of our gang spring into action. It seems that Hannah, the coonhound, can tell time! She begins that incessant baying, letting us know that it is, once again, time for all eight of us to eat.

Here's a brief description of what takes place in the kitchen.

Hannah and Casey eat first. They're on different diets, and they eat at the same time. They must eat separately so they don't eat each other's food. That's because both inhale anything that's put in front of them!

While Grandma supervises them, Aunt Lesley quickly throws together Zachary's dinner. She delivers it to him on the living room couch. That's where he spends his days because he has difficulty walking.

Once these three are taken care of, Grandma goes to the newly purchased freezer. It holds 300 pounds of ground beef just for us because of the recent dog food recall.

Now, as if she doesn't have enough to do, Grandma cooks for all of us every night so we stay healthy. While she's busy sautéing the ground beef, cooking liver, baking macaroni, and boiling rice (sounds good, doesn't it?), Aunt Lesley is escorting the rest of us into our crates to await our feasts.

Thunder won't eat if he can't find the meat! Abbey decided she preferred canned dog food after the beef arrived. (You know, the kind with the melamine in it.)

Ellie waits patiently in her crate until Thunder and Abbey clear out of the room. Then she decides whether to eat. Usually not. And never with any of that beef in her bowl. Ditto for Chloe. If there's any beef, she picks up the bowl and turns it upside down.

And that leaves me. I only eat when and if I feel like it.

After all this work, Grandma cleans the kitchen (which looks like the 3rd Army went through it). Then she waits with bated breath while Aunt Lesley checks to see who's eaten and promptly returns with a stack of half-eaten bowls. The trick is to figure out who ate what.

So, here you have it. Dinner for eight at GREYSETT every night.

And one very frustrated cook with "300 pounds" of ground beef sitting in a freezer that will take one year to pay off.

And one big, black greyhound named Thunder calling out from his crate every night, “Hey Grandma, Where’s The Beef?”

• 10 •

NOW THERE ARE HORSES

Ellie and Hannah aren't the only nervous wrecks around here lately. I've added Aunt Lesley to the group this week.

You see, since we moved to Ocala, she decided to start riding again. Mind you, our Aunt Lesley took a little hiatus (30 years' worth), but she's back in the saddle once again. And, at her age—can you imagine?

She runs around telling everyone that she rides hunters and jumpers, which she does. However, she conveniently leaves out the part about falling off the horse while going over the fence and landing flat on her back!

Ouch! Grandma had to do everything around here for a week!

Aunt Lesley rides in her first horse show this weekend in more than thirty years. She's all "FUTUTZED!!" About everything. The custom-made Italian leather boots she needed because she's so short and her calf is too wide (and they had to be sent back twice to be re-made). The Canadian wool and silk-lined show jacket. The special-order show breeches. The show helmet. Well, the list goes on and on.

Everything sits in her closet behind closed doors. A chair is in front of the closet door, and a gate is in front of her bedroom door. Why you ask? She's afraid one of us will get into her closet and chew up her boots. That's Hannah's fault. She knows how to open the closet door.

I'd give anything to be at that show this weekend (as long as she's in the ring rather than me). With all that gear on, the old girl will probably fall off. She's a nervous wreck about this show. The funniest thing is that with the fortune she'll be sporting, you'd never guess the class she was entered in: "Nervous Novice 50 Plus."

So, folks, here you have it. She can't eat. She can't sleep. Add Hannah and her maniacal baying to the scene, and she's living on Imodium and Gas-X.

Yep, that's Aunt Lesley—THE EQUESTRIAN.

I go along my merry way, staying out of trouble, except for one little slip. That big mouth, Hannah, thinks she can waltz in and steal everyone's food—and she did again. I lost my head and let her have it. No damage done, though. Just a little redirection on my part and a firm reminder as to who's the matriarch around here.

Postscript: Well, Aunt Lesley went to that show. Her trainer took one look at the Nervous Novice course and was too nervous about letting the novice ride in the Nervous Novice class. The funny thing is, all the other riders were disqualified, and Foxy (along with the foal she was carting around) could've gone into that class with or without Aunt Lesley and won the darn thing.

Oh well, that's horse shows.

• 11 •

She's Here

Well, I should have known. It was bound to happen sooner or later. Only, it didn't turn out as I thought it would. What arrived at GREYSETT wasn't another one like me–it was a horse!!!

Yep, Aunt Lesley went out and rescued a three-year-old thoroughbred filly. A great-great-granddaughter of Secretariat, no less! The horse's name is Calli, and her picture has circulated the country like wildfire. The next thing I know she'll be the one with the book. Aunt Lesley keeps flaunting this horse's pedigree all over the place. What's the matter–is it better than mine?

I mean, she's really gone over the edge. Aunt Lesley has it laminated and carries it in her handbag. Mine is buried somewhere in the closet. Calli's even got her own scrapbook of 8x10 glossies prominently displayed on the coffee table. I have one page in the GREYSETT scrapbook.

Calli's boarded at a beautiful facility nearby so Aunt Lesley can visit her daily. Any decent person is sleeping at 7 a.m., including me! But she'll be riding at 7 a.m. That poor horse!

All I know is this: there are tons of halters going back and forth to the tack shop (to find the right size), hoof supplements, vitamins, fly spray, horse toys, new shoes for Calli, and the list goes on and on. I go along my undemanding way, asking for nothing more than a good cow's hoof from time to time. I'm an easy keeper.

The last conversation between Aunt Lesley and Grandma concerned plans for a new English Setter puppy to join the family. What happened? Listen, I'm all alone out here in the woods of Ocala, surrounded by four greyhounds, a baying coonhound, and a horse.

Please–SOMEBODY HELP ME.

Send some backup!

• 12 •

THE HOOF CROOK

Despite my advancing years and some health issues, life is good. I mingle amongst the group, and along with Thunder (the 105-pound greyhound), I am one of the easy keepers.

I have only one issue: that eleven-year-old greyhound, Chloe.

She's a hoof crook.

My greatest pleasure in life is a good chew on a fresh hoof. Sometimes a girl's got to go out, you know. But when I get back, guess what? That hoof is gone! Chloe's got it! Just when it was getting nice and ripe!

There are six of us here at present. It's not just my hoof that Chloe steals. She waits in the wings, quietly, until one of us diverts our attention, and then she makes her move.

She's got a whole collection. But is she happy?

NO!

It must be the thrill of the swipe that turns her on. Once Chloe is done with a hoof, she's eyeing the next one! Grandma has to buy out PetSmart on a weekly basis.

Vacuuming in our house is quite a scene. It can't begin until fifty hooves are picked up. And, I don't know about your house, but in ours, once they are good and chewed, nobody wants them anymore. We only like a hoof when it's fresh.

It's when they've piled up that Grandma goes through the house broadcasting,

"What's that smell? It smells like someone had an accident! Oh, it's a hoof."

Well, it's a Saturday morning and, as usual, it's raining So, I think I'll retire to my crate. And with what else? A good hoof, of course!

Only this time, I'll have them close the door.

• 13 •

Uppers and Downers

With the onset of fall upon us, I've been in a little bit of a slump.

In other words–DEPRESSED!

No joie de vivre, no appetite, not sleeping. You get the picture.

Have you ever noticed that when you're not feeling quite up to par, and the rest of the household is doing great, it makes you feel even worse?

Aunt Lesley's to blame for that.

First, she moved that horse of hers to a new farm. Now, she's all excited that Calli will miraculously turn into a grand prix horse. Yeah, right.

Second, Casey and Zachary crossed The Rainbow Bridge a few months ago. Aunt Lesley went into a depression. (I can understand this one.)

So, she had to have something to sleep with—and what did she do? She adopted an eight-year-old little beagle named Milo.

Now her void is filled. She's happy again.

The beagle is cute (although he's not the English Setter puppy they promised me). But at least he stays out of my way.

With all this lousy joy going on, I feel crummy. So... I've decided that I'm just not going to eat!

Enter Grandma.

She hauls me off to the vet.

He promptly decides to put me on an antidepressant to lift my spirits and increase my appetite. I didn't want to take it, but Grandma put it in a pill pocket. I love those things!

I swear I didn't know what I was taking. (Try saying that one to the cops!)

Well, it worked. My spirits lifted. Once again, the sun rose. The birds began to sing (a little too flowery?). And I began to eat. All kidding aside, I guess I've got a good vet because I do feel better.

Our vet usually does have a solution for most of Grandma's problems. Ever heard of Benadryl?

Abbey doesn't like to be crated in the middle of the day if Aunt Lesley and Grandma go out. I don't know why. The rest of us don't mind.

But Abbey thinks she's queen and begins to howl. And that sets off everyone else. All start howling, one by one, right down the line.

Well, everyone except me, that is. I know better!

When this happens, Grandma comes in, yelling at everyone, armed with her bottle of Benadryl. She knows it'll calm them down so she can leave the house in a relatively peaceful state.

The stuff really works. But I don't need those downers.

I'm on uppers. And I feel great.

• 14 •

Couldn't Keep My Mouth Shut

Well, I have only myself to blame for this disaster.

I was lounging outside in the sun, minding my own business, when suddenly I spotted a stray in the woods on the property. Nothing unusual.

So, I began to bark. It came out of the woods and onto the driveway, and I did my usual–I went ballistic! Out runs Grandma to shut me up, and what's on the other side of the fence but a beagle!

Why couldn't it have been something like a coyote?

We have them out here, you know.

Of course, Grandma is thinking if Aunt Lesley sees this, it's all over!! She just adopted a beagle–Milo. Well, luck was not with me because with all my commotion, out runs Aunt Lesley, and in comes the beagle.

One, two, three. BAM!

He's got a name (Connor)–why, it took longer than that to name me–and he's off to the vet. Turns out, best guess, he's about seven months old (God help me) and weighs nineteen pounds. He's another tricolor, just like Milo.

Poor Grandma–she never had a chance.

I hate him. Milo hates him. And Chloe went into such a severe depression that Grandma had to take her to the vet. She was afraid that Chloe was on her last legs at twelve years old. False alarm.

It turns out, Chloe can't stand Connor either.

All I know is that our household was quiet (except for Hannah's baying). At least she doesn't tear around the house like a lunatic. Milo may be a beagle, but he is quiet and a senior like the rest of us. This new one showed up here with no collar, no tags, no nothing.

I know. Someone must have planted Connor here to punish me in my old age.

Aunt Lesley hasn't been able to sit down trying to protect all of us from him. She says she loves him, and it will keep her young. Yeah, right.

Last night, Connor went too far. I walked into my crate, and he had the gall to walk right into it after me—with me in it!

"WHAT'S THE MATTER WITH YOU?"

"DON'T YOU KNOW WHO I AM AROUND HERE?"

Aunt Lesley came running in fast–and Connor flew out of that crate fast. And not under his own power! He hasn't been back since.

So, that's my tale of woe. If I'd kept my mouth shut, Connor probably would have wandered off, and Aunt Lesley wouldn't have been the wiser.

But then again, I suppose she did save another life. Especially a lost baby.

Unfortunately, for me, he's a pain in the YOU KNOW WHAT.

• 15 •

What's This

There are so many changes going on around here.

I can't keep up.

Now, I'm really confused. At nine o'clock on a Monday morning, the telephone rings, and Grandma answers hearing that an English Setter puppy has been turned into the Humane Society.

The pup is in desperate need of veterinary care.

The Humane Society folks wanted to know if Grandma wanted to come down and rescue her before they determined how to proceed.

Well, we all know that Grandma wasted no time!

She and Aunt Lesley informed me that an English Setter puppy was finally coming—but I thought they pulled a fast one. When they walked through the door, I did a double-take. It looked like a three-month-old version of me.

In my summer clip!

In other words, she had no hair!

This new dog was pure white with tri-color markings on her ears only. Grandma and Aunt Lesley know I hate anything under the age of eight. Why did they let that thing in here?

Now, there's literally a changing of the guards at the gate to the dog room.

One of us gets let out as the other one gets let in. Whatever happened to my freedom? Now we need a rotation schedule.

And, to top things off, she sleeps across from me, so every time I open my eyes, she's looking at me. She thinks I'm her mother! It's like looking in the mirror and seeing yourself thirteen years ago.

How depressing!

Grandma named her Sophie, and she stops traffic wherever she goes.

HUH!

People want to know if she's some special breed of dog. She should live so long. She's nothing but a combination of "ME" and who knows what else.

All I know is that Grandma's thrilled because she finally has what she refers to as "her English Setter without hair - no trimming required."

And every other word out of their mouths is, "look how perfect her parts are!"

I can't win.

• 16 •

Stretch is Loose

Our household includes more than dogs and that horse!

It's also home to three canaries—and a lovebird who would like to be a canary. Allow me to set the stage.

Caruso and Julio are male canaries, and they each possess a beautiful singing voice. Another canary was purchased (by guess who) with the hope there would be a third beautiful singer—I guess to form a trio.

Aunt Lesley named the new feathered addition Enrique. One evening while she was sitting at the computer, Grandma called in announcing that "Enrique" had just laid three eggs!

Well, "he" was promptly renamed Roberta. No song. Just eggs.

Then there's Stretch—the lovebird. He's been here the longest. With every breath, he tries to mimic the canaries' songs; however, all that comes out is a loud squawk.

Keep trying, Stretch.

Thunder has lived in the same house with Stretch for a year and a half and just now realized it. Now, he won't leave the poor bird alone. He isn't smart enough to know that one doesn't mess around with Stretch. He's not a friendly bird.

Yesterday, they were both sitting in the kitchen, Aunt Lesley suddenly looked up, and there was Stretch. He was perched on top of the cabinets—free as a bird.

We were all rushed into our crates (for Stretch's safety), and all doors were closed (to limit escape routes). And Grandma ran to get "THE NET."

As she ran through the house after Stretch, with feathers flying everywhere, Aunt Lesley ran even faster in front of her trying to clear a path so she shouldn't trip.

At last, all of them exhausted, Stretch was back in his cage. And he was mad at the world. You see, he'd had a taste of freedom, and now he wanted out!

The trouble is, Thunder wants in!

Stretch has had a complete personality change for the worse. He's become even more aggressive, poking his beak out of the bars of his cage as far as he can. And Thunder keeps taunting him, night and day. And he's gotten so close that he's almost had his nose removed.

My, my. Maybe Stretch needs a couple of those "downers" that Grandma hands out occasionally.

• 17 •

You Want the Bottle?

My, how time flies.

It seems like only yesterday when the words "I'm getting that collar" bellowed from Grandma's lips to my ears every time I opened my mouth. I was just a pup back then.

Well, I finally get to sit back and listen to the new catchphrase around the house. And for once, it's not directed towards me!

You see, cute little Sophie now weighs in at forty-five pounds. She is tearing the place apart and stealing everyone's toys. Especially those infamous cow hooves!

The only way Grandma could figure out how to control her was with a squirt of water from a plastic bottle. You know, the darn thing works! Now, she threatens all of them with it. Anyone who doesn't toe the line. SQUIRT!!

Thus, the phrase "You want the bottle?"

It's a constant fixture at her side. She should wear a holster!

So far, I'm squirt-free. Well, I must be honest here. Grandma hasn't used it on the greyhounds yet, and Aunt Lesley won't let her near her precious beagle, Milo.

But, Hannah, the coonhound? Boy, oh boy–has she gotten it. Yes sir.

Sophie and Hannah. Both victims of "THE BOTTLE."

So now, as I calmly spend my days sleeping on the couch, I sometimes think back to that phrase, "Want the collar?" And

I laugh to myself because I see myself, thirteen years ago, in Sophie, the English Setter crossbreed puppy.

But there's something I don't quite get.

How come I was always going to get it with that bark collar—and Sophie gets it with that squirt bottle?

• 18 •

WALMART, CHARGE IT

Aunt Lesley's been suffering from a bad back for two weeks.

It's all because of that half-breed, Sophie.

Thunder taught her how to dig holes in the yard. Considering she now has the size and strength of an ox, she's going to town! The holes are so deep. You'd think she's mining for Tanzanite!

Our once-lush lawn now looks like a minefield. Soon it will be looking like a... Well, words fail me.

Grandma sent Aunt Lesley to Walmart to purchase cement patio stones. She wants the gardener to place them over the holes once he's filled them in.

Aunt Lesley dutifully complied and sped off to Walmart. She had twenty large stones loaded into the car along with several rolls of four-foot wire fencing.

Now, here comes the reason for the bad back.

Once home, Aunt Lesley was in her usual rush to get to the barn, and all the supplies were in the car. The gardener was coming at 5 p.m., so the supplies needed to be out of the car. She was too stubborn to wait for help.

What did she do? She unloaded the whole thing herself!

Guess who's flat on her back now?

Aunt Lesley is one prize package.

Everything must be her way or no way. Who got the short end of the stick here? Calli, that's who got it. Because of Aunt Lesley's stupidity, she hasn't been able to ride for two weeks, and her horse misses her.

Grandma keeps reminding her, in that motherly way, that if she had listened to her the first time, she'd be at the barn. That's where Aunt Lesley really wants to be instead of in bed on drugs!

As for Sophie, she keeps on digging everywhere she can find to dig.

Now the gardener picks up stones for them from Walmart.

And Grandma's words?

"Charge It!"

• 19 •

NO!!!

"NO!!!"

That seems to be the word-of-the-day around the GREYSETT household these days. That term is used on occasion for all the seniors.

Take Chloe. She's been crying for eight years. Now, when she won't stop and gets on Grandma's one remaining nerve, she warrants a "NO."

Then there's Hannah. She sits and bays for more food, even though she's already had three times her daily quota. She gets a "NO."

When Sophie's running through the house with Grandma's sheepskin-lined slippers from LL Bean, that commands a "NO!!!" When she gets hold of Calli's girth, that definitely calls for a big "NO!!!"

When she's hassling Milo (even though he's giving it right back to her), Sophie gets a "NO!!!" But not Milo. Nobody messes with Aunt Lesley's precious beagle.

As for me, I haven't heard that word uttered to me in years. Come to think of it, I haven't heard much of anything lately. You see, I'm a little hard of hearing.

So, I prefer to believe that the only words they say to me are "good girl" and "come here." But if I'm lying on my bad side, I can't hear anything.

You know the expression, "ignorance is bliss?" I believe in that!

• 20 •

THE OLD AND THE RESTLESS

Sophie's taken a particular liking to Milo.

He was rescued with a steel plate in his thigh. And he's the only one in the house who even comes close to Sophie in size, so she constantly baits him. This aggravates Milo to no end.

Since he is rather "alpha" in personality, he gives it right back to her. This constant back-and-forth teasing goes on all day long, or at least until Sophie decides to find a spot somewhere to lie down and pass out. Then Milo gets a reprieve.

Another target of Sophie's affections is Thunder.

He towers over her, but that doesn't stop her for a minute. She grabs him by the collar and doesn't seem to care if she's got a little throat along with it. Come to think of it, neither does he.

Thunder may be the most enormous greyhound on record. He's undoubtedly the sweetest. However, he's not the sharpest tool in the shed. Maybe that's why Grandma and Aunt Lesley love him so much.

Of the remaining menagerie, there is only one other so-called "pal" that Sophie tries to hang around with. That's Chloe.

Now Chloe, at her advanced age, is rather frail and looks as if she could go at any time even though she is healthy. For some reason that Grandma and Aunt Lesley can't figure out, Chloe seems to enjoy Sophie's playful "attacks."

Not only can't they understand this relationship, but they also can't comprehend where Chloe gets the energy to come to life! After five minutes of horsing around with Sophie, Chloe looks as if she is going to collapse from over-exertion–and Grandma comes running to her rescue.

So, there you have it.

Three oldie goldies and one restless youth.

Thank God Sophie has brains enough to leave me alone.

• 21 •

The Zipper Queen

I was fast asleep in my crate.

Suddenly I was awakened by the sound of Grandma's voice bellowing from the living room. At the ungodly hour of 7 a.m. The reason for the scream and the focus of the screamer–you guessed it–Sophie!!

Grandma walked into the living room and found her perched atop the couch. She had a mouthful of stuffing from one of the back cushions.

Trapped like a rat!

Apparently, Sophie has a thing for zippers. That's how she managed to remove the stuffing from the couch—she ate the zipper.

Many zippers have preceded this one.

It's been zippers on all the dog beds. Zippers on jackets, bathrobes, and handbags (designer ones). Snaps. Buttons. Hooks. Latches. Nothing is safe. Not even those cow hooves!

The only things still safe in this house are Aunt Lesley's riding boots. That's because they are high in the closet. So high that Aunt Lesley needs a ladder to reach them!

I must say, Aunt Lesley's always one step ahead of Sophie, at least when it comes to her personal belongings. She keeps everything under lock and key. And Sophie knows this. Even though she is always looking in Aunt Lesley's room, she can never find anything.

Grandma is a different story. As far as she's concerned, we come first. She's always in a rush, and she usually doesn't take the time to put her things out of Sophie's reach. Grandma is the one with the missing zippers, snaps, buttons, toeless slippers, et cetera.

And Sophie knows this, too. It's a feast in Grandma's room and famine in Aunt Lesley's.

All I know is that I came to Ocala to rest.

And ever since Sophie arrived, I haven't had a minute's peace!

Now she's eight months old and weighs sixty pounds. She shows no signs of slowing down in the growth department either.

She must be an English Setter/Godzilla cross.

Grandma has raised a lot of puppies in her day, but Sophie takes the cake!

The newest phrase around the GREYSETT household these days is, “No More Puppies!”

I can only hope and pray that they mean it this time...

EPILOGUE

So, here you have it–my story.

It is the story of the GREYSETT household throughout MY LIFETIME.

And it's the story about the agony and the ecstasy that Aunt Lesley, Grandma, and all the others put me through every single day.

How I've managed to survive this long is a mystery to me. But do you remember that old saying about the Timex watch? That's me!

I've been privy to a lot of changes around here. While the names and faces may have changed, there remain two constants in my life.

First, Grandma, who loves me and takes care of me. And then Aunt Lesley, who is still that thorn in my side. I must admit, though, that after thirteen years, I have managed to grow on her, at least a little.

I've seen new life brought into the world when litters were born (thank God they weren't mine!!).

I've seen new species arrive (horses.)

But most important of all, I've retired to Ocala–The Horse Capital of the World.

What I'm doing here, I don't exactly know. It was all Grandma's idea. What I do know is that Aunt Lesley calls our house "The Happy House."

On the other hand, I think of it as "The Nut House," which should be perfectly understandable to all if you have finished my book.

Now, turn the page to see

What's Coming Next

in the

My Dogs Talk Series

COMING NEXT — SOPHIE TALKS

Available in early 2023!

QR Quick Links

Lesley Osborn on LinkedIn

See Lesley's content

Email Subscriber Signup

Sign up to be notified when Lesley publishes a new book

Lesley Osborn Canine Consulting

Website on Computer or Mobile

Lesley Osborn Canine Consulting

Company Page on LinkedIn

FREE 20-minute Consultation Call

with Lesley Osborn • *No Obligation*

About LOCC

Lesley Osborn Canine Consulting provides education and guidance on fostering, adopting, and caring for adult, senior, and special needs dogs

The guiding principle: **providing loving forever homes to rescue and shelter dogs**. Lesley has shared the last 4+ decades of her life caring for rescued dogs, especially seniors.

"***QUALITY OF THEIR LIVES***" will always be at the forefront of Lesley's work.

The bonds between dogs and *their people* are reciprocal—these bonds help the physical and emotional well-being of all.

Having dogs as members of your family should never be considered a job. To be loved unconditionally is a privilege.

Dogs raised with kindness, a soft voice, and a gentle hand = sweet-natured members of your family. There are ongoing challenges in meeting the ever-changing needs of your canine family.

Lesley provides insight into gentle yet effective ways to address these needs.

Lesley Osborn is *not* a veterinarian. However, she will always have the best interest of your dog in mind.

Based on decades of experience, Lesley may recommend that you consider a consultation with your veterinarian. Not all issues require consultation. And should you want additional advice, Lesley can offer a list of questions you can ask your vet.

To schedule a **FREE 20-minute Consultation Call** with Lesley, scan the QR code below.

A Special Message from Lesley

Adopting vs Shopping

All dogs deserve loving homes, regardless of where they come from.

Adopt, don't shop is a standard some deem absolute. I agree with the principle—but there's more to consider.

Many responsible people are dog breeders. When a litter is born not all pups are deemed fit for the show ring in the breeder's opinion. These pups are often reserved for those looking for a pure-breed dog as a family companion.

A responsible breeder may not feel a particular pup's conformation is appropriate to represent their show line. Much work in the genetic planning of future litters in the dog show world goes on behind the scenes.

Breeders who work like this are good people, who care about the placement of their pups.

On the flip side, many show dogs will be looking for loving homes after their show careers are over. Responsible breeders look for the perfect home for these canines to spend their golden years in surrounded by love with a family outside the ring.

And on the following, I speak from experience. I had two show senior English Setters that had been thrown over a fence—no longer wanted.

Guess where they came to live?

GREYSETT!

These are a few of the reasons pure-breed dogs find themselves in shelters.

This is the reason for breed-specific rescue groups. Check these groups and it's not uncommon to find mixed breeds in these rescue groups.

Be careful with your words. Not all breeders are "puppy mills." Reputable breeders care about their dogs and where they are placed from birth through retirement.

Thanks for reading Tia Talks

Lesley

Forever Home

www.ingramcontent.com/pod-product-compliance
Ingram Content Group UK Ltd.
Pitfield, Milton Keynes, MK11 3LW, UK
UKHW021401070726
13610UKWH00012B/65

9 798987 480700